Wacky Water Fun With Science

OTHER McGRAW-HILL BOOKS BY ED SOBEY

Fantastic Flying Fun with Science

Just Plane Smart

Car Smarts: Activities for the Open Road

Wrapper Rockets and Trombone Straws: Science at Every Meal

WACKY WATER FUN WITH SCIENCE

Science you can float, sink, squirt, and sail

Ed Sobey, Ph.D.

Illustrated by Bill Burg

McGraw-Hill

New York San Francisco Washington, D.C. Auckland Bogotá
Caracas Lisbon London Madrid Mexico City Milan
Montreal New Delhi San Juan Singapore
Sydney Tokyo Toronto

McGraw-Hill

A Division of The **McGraw-Hill** *Companies*

1 2 3 4 5 6 7 8 9 0   DOC / DOC   9 0 9 8 7 6 5 4 3 2 1 0 9

ISBN   0-07-134809-3

This book was set in Caecilia Roman by Jaclyn J. Boone.

Printed and bound by R.R. Donnelley & Sons.

Solution to the
Crossword Puzzle Glossary

To Professor Ray Waldner,
as wet and wacky a character
as you'd ever want to meet

Contents

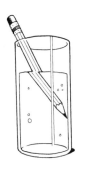

~ PART THREE ~
BUILDING BOATS, SUBS, WATER WHEELS, & MORE

~ PART ONE ~
GETTING YOUR BEARINGS

Launching on a sea of exploration

Messing around with model boats, waterwheels, and pumps is a great way to spend the day. You can try out activities at home, the beach, the pool, or school. As you set sail for fun, you'll learn the science behind all things wet.

How many ways can you propel a boat? We've provided lots, but you can probably think of several more once you've tried these. Make a pump to lift water? Sounds hard? You can do it in minutes once you have the technology (know-how) and the materials. You'll probably invent a new way once you've built ours. Bend light or make a magnifying glass using water? It's a cinch.

The idea here is that you have fun and learn when you use your mind and your hands together. Start with the projects here and then develop your own methods and ideas. And, ask lots of questions along the way.

We've divided the activities into two types. The first are neat science demonstrations you can do for yourself or as part of a science show. Second are projects you can build.

To help you navigate the science, we've provided navigational aids. These are road signs that tell you at a glance what the underlying science is. We've included some to show which projects would be great for science fairs. You can find these signs explained on the following pages.

Also, meet Wilbur the loon. Loons fly, float, and dive, and have a wacky laugh that seems to travel miles across a lake. They are the most colorful characters of northern lakes. It must be fun to be a loon.

You can find navigational aids, along with Wilbur, in this book and in its companion, *Fantastic Flying Fun with Science* which has lots of building projects you can fly, spin, launch, and ride through the air. So "wilburize" yourself by getting ready for the fun of making stuff that floats, sinks, squirts, and sails.

Surface tension

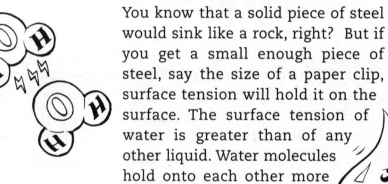

You know that a solid piece of steel would sink like a rock, right? But if you get a small enough piece of steel, say the size of a paper clip, surface tension will hold it on the surface. The surface tension of water is greater than of any other liquid. Water molecules hold onto each other more strongly than molecules of other liquids.

Pressure

Change the pressure just a bit and water moves up a straw, or defies gravity, or makes it really hard to blow bubbles. Pressure results from piling up the air above us in the sky and piling up water in a lake, pool, or ocean. There's lots more pressure at the bottom of a pile than on top.

Density

Would you rather carry a bucket of air or water. Water is much denser than air, so a bucket of water weighs lots more. You can change the density of water by heating or cooling it, or by adding stuff to it, like salt. Cold, salty water is denser than warm, fresh water and falls to the bottom of an ocean or bucket. Density means the weight divided by the volume of space it takes up. That's dense, man.

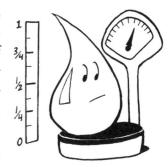

Light

Why don't submarines have windows? Although sounds travel far underwater, light doesn't. If you're in the clearest water you can see about 200 feet; but you can hear sounds from miles away. Both sound and light bend in water which makes for some interesting effects.

When water bends light, you can see things backwards, larger, or broken. Take a look.

3

Buoyancy

Why do ships sink? They loose their buoyancy. Ships are holes in the ocean that keep the water out. If you let the ocean inside, ships sink. Like a rock. Because ships, including all the air inside, are lighter than the water they push out of the way, they float. If you replace the air with water, ships are no longer lighter than water. Blub, blub, blub and down she goes.

Stored energy

Want to make a boat move? You need to supply some energy and store it until you're ready to get underway. You can store it as air pressure in a balloon, chemical energy in a battery, or the energy of stretching a rubber band. Another way to store energy is to hold water behind a dam. That energy is converted into electricity by having it turn turbines. While you're thinking about storing energy, eat a cookie to store some energy in your body. Happy floating, sinking, squirting, and sailing.

Converting fun experiments into science fair projects

Is it science fair time? Does that bring a smile to your face, or a frown? Science is learning by investigating and is fun, so our first goal is making sure your science fair project will be fun. Why? Because if your project turns into drudgery, you're less likely to do a good job. You'll find other things to do instead of working on your project. If you pick a topic you really like, you'll work harder, learn more, and end up with a better science fair entry.

Many of the projects in this book lend themselves to science fair projects. Where we have seen obvious project possibilities, we've pointed them out. Look for Wilbur.

To convert one of the projects in this book to a science fair topic, you will need to:

1. **Build and play with the floaters, sinkers, squirters, and sailers and ask questions about them** You might be intrigued to know how they work or how far they can travel. Maybe you can find a better design to use or a new experiment to try. Whatever questions you come with, write them in your science fair notebook. If you're having trouble coming up with questions, bring in some friends, members of your family, or your teacher. Show them what you've made and see if they can suggest topics for study.

2. **Keep messing around** Messing around with boats and things wet is how good science and inventing are done. Many great inventions arose when people played around with things that caught their attention. You can imagine people thinking of a boat that would travel submerged, and then trying to make one. Until they did, other people wouldn't believe it. The more you play with your device, the more neat stuff you'll notice and the more ideas you'll get. While you play, keep thinking about the questions you raised, and see what other questions come to your mind.

3. **Pick a question** You may have lots of questions, but you've got to focus on one for the science fair. You can work on the others later. What makes a good question? You will want to pick one that will let you do some experiments that give you numerical results.

As an example, you could compare how far a rubber band powered boat travels as you increase the number of twists in the rubber band (see page 62). You could count the number of turns you give the rubber band and then measure how far the boat goes.

To show your data, make a graph. On the horizontal axis show the number of turns. Plot the distance traveled on the vertical axis.

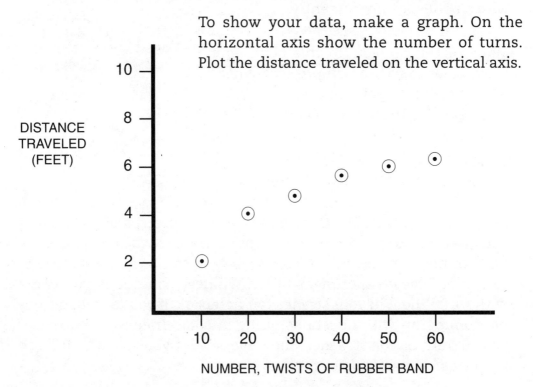

DISTANCE TRAVELED (FEET)

NUMBER, TWISTS OF RUBBER BAND

The pattern of the data points tell a story about the physics of propelling boats with rubber bands and an interesting story makes the basis for a good science fair project.

You want to choose a question that you will be able to answer in time for the science fair. Also, you will need to do some library research so you need a topic that you can find in books, research journals, magazines, on the INTERNET, or in video tapes. The librarian at your school or public library can help you find resources.

Of course you want to pick a question that's going to provide you with an experiment that will be fun to do.

4. **Follow the guidelines** Make sure you understand how the science fair expects you to conduct your experiments and show your results.

5. **Run your experiments** In the example of the rubber band powered boat, you would want to repeat tests three or more times for the same number of twists of the rubber band. You would add the distances together and divide by the number of tests you made to give you the average distance. Use the average distance for the data you plot in a graph.

6. **Take some pictures** Take pictures of building and testing your device. They can give your presentation board a polished appearance.

7. **Look at your data graph and see what story it tells** Does the boat travel farther when you twist the rubber band more? If it did, could you draw a straight line to connect all the data points? If a straight line wouldn't connect the points, what shape line would? If the points are scattered all over the graph, what does that tell you? See if you can figure out what story the graph tells, and if that makes sense with your understanding of the physics involved. If you can't figure it out, get some expert help at your school, a local high school, or a college. Keep asking questions until you understand.

8. **Write up the analysis and make your presentation** Reread the guidelines so you will create a presentation board and report that the science fair officials expect.

On the presentation board you will want to include photographs, the graphs of data, and the text and labels. If permitted, display any devices you made in front of the board.

Did we leave out anything out? Yes. Check those guidelines again. You may need to get your project approved before you start your experiments, but first need to do some experiments to figure out what your project is going to be. So get started early so you have time to pick your project and do the library research on time.

Most of all, pick a project that you like and have fun. Science and inventing is supposed to be fun. Make sure your experience is.

8

~ PART TWO ~
WET & WILD DEMONSTRATIONS

Sticky water

OVERVIEW Amaze your friends by showing them how sticky your water is. But, it's low pressure, not stickiness, that holds the ball.

MATERIALS
- a ping pong ball
- 2' long piece of string
- duct tape
- bath tub or deep sink

PROCEDURES 1. With a small square of duct tape, attach the string to a ping pong ball.

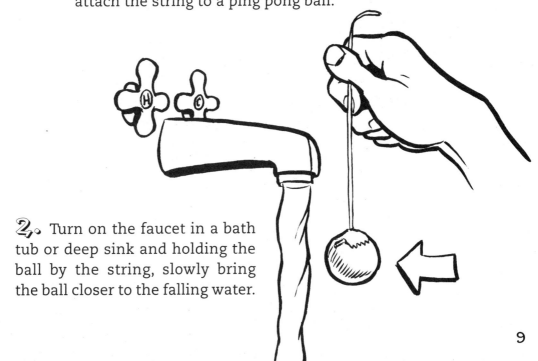

2. Turn on the faucet in a bath tub or deep sink and holding the ball by the string, slowly bring the ball closer to the falling water.

ACTION

The stream grabs the ball and holds it.
You can feel how hard the water stream holds it
when you pull on the string to get the ball out.

DEMONSTRATION TIP

❖ *Tell your friends that your house has really sticky water.*
It's so sticky that it will hold a ball and not let go.
They of course won't believe you, so you'd better show them.

WHAT'S HAPPENING? Fast moving water creates lower pressure. Higher pressure on one side of the ball pushes it toward the lower pressure of the stream.

SO WHAT? Next time you take a shower where there is a shower curtain, check out how the curtain hangs before you turn on the water. Then, turn on the water and watch the curtain get sucked inward. Fast falling water from the shower pulls air in from the sides taking the bottom of the curtain with it.

More sticky water

OVERVIEW Make water stick together or break apart, with a flick of your fingers.

MATERIALS • an empty 2-liter plastic bottle, milk carton, or jug
  • a nail
  • water

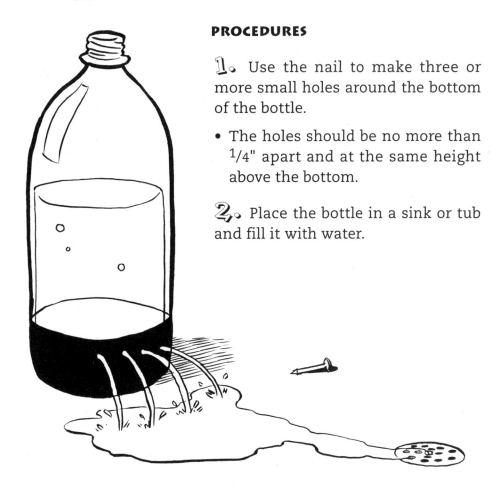

PROCEDURES

1. Use the nail to make three or more small holes around the bottom of the bottle.

• The holes should be no more than 1/4" apart and at the same height above the bottom.

2. Place the bottle in a sink or tub and fill it with water.

ACTION

Water comes out of the holes as individual streams. However, you can stick two of them together by pinching them between your forefinger and thumb. Once you've stuck two together, see if you can stick on a third. To unstick the streams, pass a finger in front of the holes in the bottle.

IF IT DOESN'T WORK

Do you get individual streams of water from the holes? If not, you may have the holes too close together. If you get individual streams but can't stick them together, the holes are too far apart.

WHAT'S HAPPENING?

The surface tension of the water holds the streams together, once you bring them together. When you interrupt the streams you separate them into individual streams again.

What else?

◎ Try making more holes spaced slightly farther apart.
See how far apart you can make the holes
and still get the water to stick together.

Pepper break out

3

OVERVIEW It's a mad dash to the sides of the glass — for all the flecks of pepper, once you've reduced the surface tension.

MATERIALS
- a glass
- water
- pepper
- a spoon
- dish washing liquid

PROCEDURES

1. Fill the glass with water and drop some pepper on top. It spreads out evenly across the surface.

2. Use the end of the spoon to pick up a small dab of dish washing liquid from the nozzle.

3. Touch the end of the spoon with the dish washing liquid to the surface of the water at the center.

13

RESULTS

The pepper flees to the edges of the glass. It has scattered!

WHAT'S HAPPENING?

Imagine that you spread the pepper onto an inflated balloon. Then, in slow motion, you broke the balloon right in the center of the pepper. The pepper would move away from the break. In the water experiment you just did the same thing without the balloon. When you added the dab of soap, you reduced the surface tension of the water in the center. Water and pepper moved quickly to the outside where surface tension was still strong.

SO WHAT?

Reducing surface tension is the role soap plays in washing stuff.

Soap reduces the surface tension of water so it can flow under dirt and lift it away. It also lets you blow enormous bubbles. Try that in Project 5.

Make steel float

OVERVIEW Everyone knows that steel sinks in water, right? You can demonstrate that steel floats.

MATERIALS
- a clear bowl
- box of paper clips (large ones are easier to use)
- water
- soap or liquid dish detergent

PROCEDURES

1. Fill the bowl with water, almost to the rim.

2. Unbend a paper clip to make a right angle.

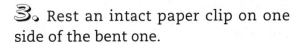

3. Rest an intact paper clip on one side of the bent one.

- Hold the other side of the bent clip and slowly lower it into the water.

- The second paper clip will float and you will be able to move the bent one down and away.

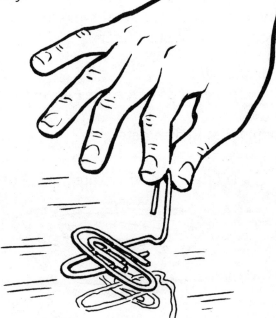

IF IT DOESN'T WORK

If the paper clip fell to the bottom, try it again but first rinse the bowl and the bent paper clip, and use a different paper clip to float. Something in the water or on the first paper clip reduced the surface tension. Also, this doesn't work if you drop the paper clip or put one end in before the other. You have to lay it flat on the water.

RESULTS   The paper clip is floating; so, steel floats! How did you do that?

WHAT'S HAPPENING?

When we say something floats we mean that the object displaces more pounds of water than it weighs. Something that has a density greater than water sinks; so why does the paper clip, made of steel stay on the surface? Surface tension of the water holds it up. That is, water molecules are holding onto each other so strongly that the paper clip doesn't fall through. Look at the water's surface from the side and you will see that the paper clip is pushing the surface down.

SO WHAT?   Water surface tension allows water strider bugs to zip across a pond without falling in, and keeps even high density objects, like a steel paper clip, on the surface as long as the objects are small. Try the demonstration with a penny and you won't be able to get it to stay on the surface. It's too heavy for surface tension to hold it.

DEMONSTRATION TIP

❖ *So if surface tension holds the paper clip, what happens if you decrease the surface tension? The paper clip will sink to the bottom. How do you decrease the surface tension? You do it the same way you clean your hands, use some soap. Once the paper clip is floating, take the other clip and rub it on the nozzle of the bottle of dish washing liquid. Just get a tiny bit of soap on the clip and lower it slowly to touch the surface of the water as far from the floating clip as you can. As soon as you touch the surface, the floating paper clip will sink.*

DO IT AGAIN   You'll have to rinse out the bowl to get rid of all traces of the soap, or the paper clips won't float on the surface.

5 Bubbles galore!

OVERVIEW You can reduce surface tension and make water wetter by adding soap, and then blowing it into bubbles

MATERIALS
- 1 rinsed out gallon milk jug with screw-on lid
- 10 cups water
- 1 cup of Joy liquid dish detergent
- 4 tablespoons glycerin (available in drug stores)
- cookie sheet
- string
- straws
- cardboard tubes or Styrofoam cups
- coated paper plates
- scissors

PROCEDURES

1. Pour 10 cups of water into the milk jug.

2. Add one cup of Joy liquid dish detergent and 4 tablespoons of glycerin. (You can skip the glycerin, but it tends to make the bubbles last longer.)

- Now you have enough bubble solution for many afternoons of fun.

- This formula is the A.C. Gilbert's Discovery Village Bubble Solution; check out their web page at: www.acgilbert.org.

ACTION   Pour some bubble solution into a shallow pan. A cookie sheet works well. To make great bubbles, create you own bubble wands, or build the ones listed on pages 20 – 22.

WHAT'S HAPPENING?

The detergent reduces the surface tension of the water allowing the water molecules to stretch farther apart. Once you've captured air under some bubble solution, the surface tension contracts around the air to form a sphere (if its floating in air) or hemisphere (on the cookie sheet). These shapes result from the surface tension holding the water molecules together — a sphere takes the least surface area to hold a volume of air.

TRY THIS   Take a straw and hold one end in the pan with bubble juice. Blow some bubbles. If you poke a bubble with another straw, one that hasn't been dipped in bubble juice, you'll break the bubble. If you use a straw that is wet, you will be able to push it into the bubble without breaking it. You can stick you finger through a bubble, as long as your finger is wet. If any part is dry, the bubble will break when the dry part hits the bubble.

POP IT   A bubble pops because the air pressure inside is greater than in the air outside. Surface tension pulls the water molecules closer which compresses the bubble surface and increases the air pressure inside. When you make a hole in a bubble, you release the pressure. As the air rushes out, it breaks up the bubble, sending bubble juice flying.

Big bubbles

See how big a bubble you can make. Blow a few bubbles in the pan, and then pull the straw out. Pick one bubble and jab the straw inside without letting the juice from the pan inside the bubble. Blow gently to make the largest bubble you can.

Bigger bubbles

Find the cardboard tube within a roll of paper towels. Or, use a paper cup and poke a hole in the bottom so you can blow through it. Dip one end into the bubble solution and gently blow through the other end or the narrow opening. Launch these bubbles into the air.

Try using a kitchen funnel. Dip the wide end into the solution and blow through the narrow end.

Bubble inside bubble

Try blowing a bubble inside a bubble.
After blowing a few bubbles in the pan, pull out the straw.
Reload the straw by dipping it in the juice, and stick it back inside a bubble and blow gently.

Bigger still

Use a metal coat hanger. If you find any sharp edges on the coat hanger, tape them so you don't get cut. Bend it into the shape of a rectangle or circle and wrap it with a thick string. The string will help hold the solution. Dip it into the juice and make sure all sides get into the juice, or you won't be able to form a bubble. Or, cut the center out of a coated paper plate, giving you a ring. Dip the ring in the bubble juice and wave it through the air.

POP!

Prevent pops

If your bubbles are breaking, it may be that they are bumping into something that is dry. Make sure the sides of your container and straw are wet. Or, the air may be too dry. Use a water mister to spray some water droplets into the air above your bubble pan.

Big bubble generator

We're talking really big bubbles. Feed a four foot long piece of string through two straws and tie the ends together. Slide the knot into one of the straws. Drop it into the juice and make sure all of it gets wet. Grab the straws in opposite hands – your hands need to be wet too – and separate the straws to reveal a sheet of bubble juice. Run backward to launch a bubble. (Guess what happens if you run forward holding the bubble generator and a sheet of bubble juice).

Here are two tricks to help you. First, get out of the way of the bubble. You might get someone to hold one straw while you hold the other. Second, to form complete bubbles, twist the strings together just before the bubble bursts. With practice you'll be able to launch huge bubbles into the air.

SCIENCE FAIR

- Run some experiments to find out what formula for bubble juice gives you the biggest bubbles.

- How will you measure the bubbles to know which are biggest? You could blow them onto a wet ruler or meter stick and read the markings on each side.

Suck it up 6

OVERVIEW   You can move water from one glass to the other without lifting either glass. Magic? No, capillary action!

MATERIALS   • a bowl
  • a glass
  • water
  • food coloring
  • paper towels

PROCEDURES

1. Fill the glass with water and add a few drops of food coloring.

2. Set the glass and bowl a few inches away from each other.

3. Twist a paper towel into a long roll and insert one end into the empty bowl.

4. Insert the other end of the towel into the full glass.
   • Make sure that the end of the paper towel is in the water.

ACTION Okay, the action isn't fast enough to arouse the interest of ESPN, but have some patience and you'll see water move up the paper towel and down into the bowl.

RESULTS In a few minutes a pool of colored water will be in the bowl.

WHAT'S HAPPENING? Water moves through the tiny openings in the paper towel. Surface tension pulls water into a narrow space and then into the next one. The food color, since it is mixed with the water, goes along for the ride and shows you the progress of the water.

What else?

◎ Try materials others than a paper towel.
  An old cotton sock or piece of a tee shirt will work well.
  Try something with a much bigger opening,
  like a drinking straw. Will that work?
  Or, materials other than cotton?

SO WHAT?

Water moves from the roots to the leaves of trees, wax moves up candle wicks, and sweat moves from your body through your tee shirt due to capillary action. By the way, what's that smell?

7   Suck it up a straw

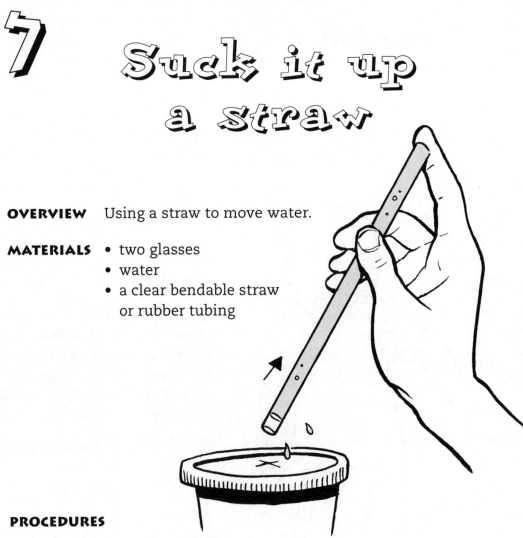

OVERVIEW   Using a straw to move water.

MATERIALS
- two glasses
- water
- a clear bendable straw or rubber tubing

PROCEDURES

1. You've done this, right?

- Dip the straw into a glass of water.
- Place your index finger on the opening on top of the straw and lift the straw out of the water.
- Presto, the water's still inside.
- You could transfer water from a full glass to an empty one, one straw-full at a time. But there's a better way.

WHAT'S HAPPENING?

What's holding the water in the straw? "Suction," you say. Yeah, but a better explanation is that air pressure is holding it. The air pressure outside the straw is greater than the pressure inside the straw, and that higher pressure pushes the water up into the straw. As soon as you let air in by moving your index finger, the pressure inside drops to the same as outside, and gravity pulls the water down. Splash.

MAKING A SIPHON

Let's move some water! Dip a bendable straw into the full glass with the top of the straw down. Draw out a straw-full of water as before. Keeping your finger on the top of the straw, bend the straw just enough so the short section is in the glass of water with the end under water. Place the longer section so it will drain into the bowl as soon as you move your finger. Let go with your finger to start the siphon.

As the water level in the glass lowers and rises in the bowl, see if you can reverse the flow through the straw. Raise the bowl and lower the glass while keeping both ends of the straw under water.

RESULTS Water is flowing through the straw siphon from the glass into the bowl.

WHAT'S HAPPENING? Water will go downhill, even if it has to go up hill to get there. When you remove your finger, water flows out one end. It can't flow out both ends because air pressure inside the straw would be reduced and the outside air pressure would hold the water inside. So when you remove your finger, water flows out one end. Which one? The lower end since there is more water pushing down on that side. Once the flow starts, water leaving the straw is replaced by more water entering the upper end, pushed by atmospheric pressure.

Chirping atomizer 8

OVERVIEW   Chirp like a bird or blow water up a straw when you reduce air pressure in a tube.

MATERIALS
- straws
- water
- a glass
- scissors

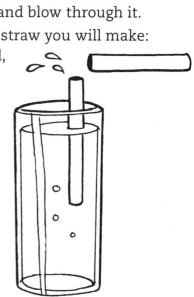

PROCEDURES   **1.**   Cut a straw in half and set aside one piece. Cut the other piece nearly in half, but don't cut all the way through the straw.

- Cut far enough so you can bend the straw where you cut it.

2.   Put one end of this straw in the glass of water and hold it vertical.

- Hold the other part horizontally and blow through it.
- As you adjust the position of the straw you will make: bubbles in the glass, a whistle, and, as you raise the straw higher, a chirping sound. Pure canary.

3. Cut the other half straw into two pieces.

- Hold one piece vertically in the glass.
- Hold the second piece horizontally, about an inch above the vertical piece.
- Blow hard through the horizontal straw.
- If you blow hard enough you'll get water to rise up the vertical straw and spray.

IF IT DOESN'T WORK Shorten the length of the part of the straw that's out of the water. Lower the other end farther into the glass. Blow harder!

WHAT'S HAPPENING? You made a whistle and an atomizer. By blowing across the top of the straw you created swirls of air that you heard as sounds of one pitch. Changing the height of the straw above the water level changes the pitch of the sound.

In the second experiment you blew across the top of the straw which lowered the air pressure in the vertical straw. Atmospheric pressure outside the straw pushed water up the straw since there was lower pressure at the top of the straw. When the water hit the fast moving air coming through the horizontal straw, it broke into tiny droplets and sprayed. That's what a perfume atomizer does: it raises the liquid by blowing air across a tube that brings up the liquid and sprays it out as a mist.

Make your own ocean   9

OVERVIEW   Okay King Neptune, you get to call the shots in your ocean. You get to mix up the waters and see where they go!

MATERIALS
- 2-liter soda bottle
- hot and cold water
- ice cubes
- small plastic bags with twist ties
- scissors
- food coloring
- white paper
- nail

PROCEDURES

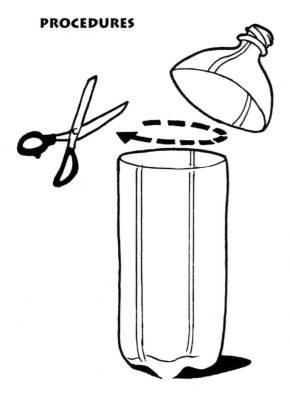

1. Every ocean needs boundaries, so first make the basin for your ocean. Cut the top off a 2-liter soda bottle.

- Cut near the top of the bottle just below where the sides start to curve in towards the neck.

2. Fill the ocean about 2/3 full of hot water from the tap.

3. Put three or four ice cubes in a plastic bag and close off the bag with a twist tie, or knot.

4. Lay the bag on top of the hot water.

5. Prop the white paper behind the bottle so you can see the results of the next step.

6. Squirt a bit of food coloring into the water along the sides of the bag.

• Watch what happens to the food coloring.

RESULTS

The coloring sank toward the bottom of the ocean.

WHAT'S HAPPENING?

The ice cooled (by touching or conduction) the water near it. As the water cooled it became more dense and so it sank. The food coloring acted liked a marker so you could see streamers of cool water falling to the bottom.

EXPERIMENT 2

Repeat the experiment, but this time let the cold water flow into the warmer ocean.

- Rinse out the ocean and refill it with warm, clear water.

- Put it in front of the white paper again.

- Mix some ice cubes and cold tap water in a plastic bag.

- Add a few drops of food coloring to the bag. Wait a few minutes so the water can cool.

- With a nail poke a small hole in the bag and immediately insert it into the bottle so the cold, colored water can flow into your warm ocean.

RESULTS The colder, denser water fell to the bottom of the ocean.

SO WHAT? The oceans and lakes cool by giving heat to the atmosphere. They lose heat when they come in contact with cooler air at the surface, when evaporation occurs, and when they radiate energy into the atmosphere and space. When water on the surface cools, it becomes more dense and sinks.

10 Make your own ocean, part II

OVERVIEW   You can change your ocean by adding water of different density at the bottom.

MATERIALS
- 2-liter soda bottle
- a funnel
- 10" of clear plastic tubing, sized to fit the end of the funnel (from a hardware store)
- duct tape
- jar for mixing water and ice

- kitchen baster
- hot and cold water
- ice cubes
- glue
- food coloring
- white paper

PROCEDURES

1. Start with the ocean container you made for the previous experiments. Add to it a device for delivering water to the bottom of the bottle: the funnel and tubing.

   • Attach the funnel to the plastic tubing. If they don't fit together snugly, secure them in place with glue or tape.

2. Use a piece of duct tape to hold the funnel to the side of the bottle so the tube touches the bottom of the bottle.

3. This time, add the cold water to the bottom of the ocean, instead of to the top.

   • Mix some ice cubes with cold tap water in a jar and add a couple of drops of food coloring. Give the mixture a few minutes to cool.

4. While the water is cooling, fill the ocean about 2/3 full of hot water from the tap.

5. With the white paper behind the bottle, slowly pour (or use a baster to transfer) cold, colored water into the funnel.

6. Watch what happens to the water coming out the end of the tubing. Hold the white paper behind the bottle and look from the front and side of the 2-liter bottle.

WET & WACKY FACTS

The oceans are salty in part because rivers carry salt to the oceans. If we used trucks to carry the same amount of salt that rivers carry, it would take 35 trucks driving by each second, forever. Be glad you don't live next to that road.

RESULTS You created a layer of cold, colored water at the bottom of the bottle. Although the cold water tends to rise above the bottom as you pour it in the bottle, it settles to the bottom. You can see the colored layer of water at the bottom and clear water above it.

CHECK IT OUT Use the baster to take a water sample from the top of the ocean and feel the temperature. It will be warm. Squeeze the bulb of the baster to empty it, and insert it to the bottom so you can take a water sample there. Squirt it on the back of your hand; the water will be cold.

WHAT'S HAPPENING?

If you leave the mixture long enough the water will come to a common temperature. But for a while the bottom will be cold and the top will be warm. The two water masses tend not to mix together; the less dense water is on top and the more dense water is on the bottom.

EXPERIMENT 2

What will happen if you do the experiment backward? No, don't stand backward and try it; add warm, colored water to the bottom of a cold, clear ocean.

- Rinse out the ocean and refill it with cold tap water and a few ice cubes.

- Put it in front of the white paper again.

- Add some hot tap water to a few drops of food coloring in a jar and mix.

- After giving the ice a few minutes to cool the water in the bottle, slowly pour (or use a baster to transfer) some warm water into the funnel.

RESULTS The warm, less dense water rose toward the top of the bottle. Shortly after you add some more warm, colored water, the entire ocean takes on a tint of color. In the previous experiment you created a colored layer at the bottom; here the color was mixed throughout the ocean.

SO WHAT? Cooling at the surface and heating from below mix the water column. In the fall, lakes cool at the surface and the surface waters sink, forcing deeper waters toward the surface. Nutrients that were trapped in the bottom layers of water are mixed throughout the water column, available for plants to use. The surface cooling creates an escalator that pulls nutrients up to the surface.

Make your own salty ocean, part III

OVERVIEW Some neat things happen when we make our ocean very stable with cold and salty water underneath and warm, fresh water on top.

MATERIALS
- 2-liter soda bottle and funnel-tubing device built in Project 10
- tablespoon
- salt
- quart jar with lid
- kitchen baster
- hot and cold water
- ice cubes
- food coloring
- white paper
- drinking straw

PROCEDURES

1. Use the ocean container you made for the previous experiments.

2. Add some ice cubes, cold tap water, and a tablespoon of salt to the quart jar.

3. Add enough food coloring to the jar to give a vibrant color.

4. Put the lid on and shake it up. Set the mixture aside for a few minutes while you get the ocean ready.

5. Fill the ocean about 2/3 full of hot water from the tap.

6. Place the white paper behind the bottle.

7. Shake the jar again and then open it.

8. Carefully pour (or use a baster to transfer) cold, salty, colored water into the funnel.

9. Watch what happens to the water coming out the end of the tubing. Watch from the side with the white paper behind the bottle.

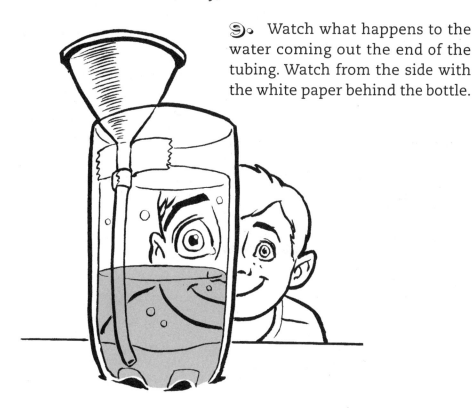

RESULTS The cold, salty water formed a pool at the bottom. After pouring in all the water it quickly settled to the bottom. This occurred even faster than in the previous experiment when you poured in cold, fresh, water. Notice that the difference in color between the bottom layer and the rest of the water column is stronger — there is a greater contrast. The salt made the cold water even more dense.

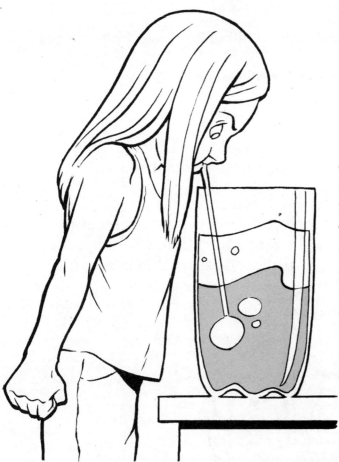

CHECK IT OUT

Insert a straw into the bottom layer and blow a few bubbles. The bubbles will cause waves to form between the two layers of water. Watch as they slowly move back and forth. Oceanographers call these "internal waves" because they occur inside the water column, not at the surface.

WHAT'S HAPPENING?

The large difference in densities of the two layers of water create a stable water column. Heavy water is on the bottom and lighter water is on top. Waves can move on the interface between any two fluids of different densities and you can see the waves moving.

CHECK IT OUT AGAIN

Dribble some cold, salty water onto the top of the ocean and watch it rapidly fall to the bottom. The shimmering you see in the water is due to light being bent as it moves through water of different densities. Divers see shimmering when diving in fjords or off the mouths of rivers where fresh and salt water mix.

EXPERIMENT 2

Try this experiment again but this time use tap water on top and warm and salty water below.

- Rinse out the ocean and refill it with warm tap water.
- Put it in front of the white paper again.
- Add a tablespoon of salt and a few drops of food coloring to a quart of warm tap water in a jar.
- Put on the lid and shake.
- Pour (or use the baster to transfer) warm, salty water into the funnel.

RESULTS

Again, you've created two layers of water. Salty (colored) water on the bottom, and warm (fresh) water on top. But notice that as you add the salty water it doesn't settle to the bottom as quickly as in the last experiment. The boundary between the two layers isn't as distinct.

WHAT'S HAPPENING?

Both temperature and the quantity of dissolved salt (called *salinity*) determine the density of water. Lower temperatures and higher salinity make more dense water. In this experiment you made water more dense by adding salt and not by cooling it. The difference in densities of the upper and lower layers weren't as great as before.

Rescue an egg

OVERVIEW   You can convince an egg to switch from being a sinker to a floater by changing the density of the water around it.

MATERIALS
- a clear glass or jar
- water
- an egg
- a spoon
- salt (lots of it)

PROCEDURES

1. Fill the glass with water.

2. Carefully add the egg by lowering it in the glass with the spoon.

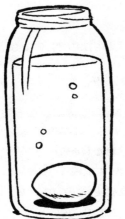

- Challenge a friend to get the egg to the surface without touching it. Although he can't, you can move the egg without touching it or changing it in any way. The trick is to make the water denser so the egg will float.

3. Start pouring in salt.

- We're not talking pinches and dabs, pour it in.

4. After you pour in enough of the salt to spice eggs for an army, swirl it around with the spoon. Make sure the salt is dissolved.

- If the egg doesn't lift off the bottom, add more salt.
- With just the right solution of salt in water, the egg will float in the middle of the water column.
- Add some more and it will bob at the surface.

WHAT'S HAPPENING?

Salt water has a higher density than fresh water does. The increased density of the salty water was enough to buoy the egg.

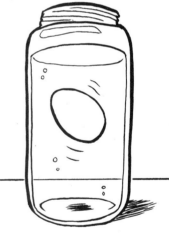

What else?

◎ Take some sugar out of a soda and what happens? Float a diet soda and a regular soda in a tub of water. One will float and one will sink. Guess which one floats.

13

Making waves

OVERVIEW You can make your own wave-viewing gizmo. Catch the waves!

MATERIALS
- 2-liter soda bottle with lid
- food coloring
- water
- vegetable oil

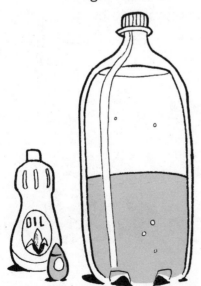

PROCEDURES

1. Fill the bottle half way with water.

2. Be generous in adding food coloring.

3. Screw on the lid, and shake the bottle.

4. Remove the lid and top off the bottle with vegetable oil.

5. Recap the lid.

44

ACTION

The oil will take up its position on top, since it is less dense than water. If you shake the bottle, the oil and water will separate soon after you stop shaking. To create waves, turn the bottle on its side.

RESULTS

You've made an internal wave gizmo.

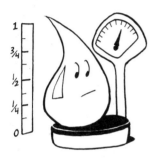

WHAT'S HAPPENING

Surface waves are the ones you see on the surface of the ocean or the top of a glass of milk when someone bumps it. *Internal waves* occur between two fluids that have different densities, like oil and water. Check out how slowly the wave moves from end to end.

What else?

◎ By picking different liquids you can change how slowly or quickly the internal waves move. The greater the difference in densities is, the faster the internal waves will move.

◎ You could remake your wave-viewing gizmo using salty water with food coloring and oil to get faster waves. Adding the salt will increase the density of the water.

◎ Or, try adding salt to the oil to reduce the difference in densities. Instead of using vegetable oil, try using syrup and water in your gizmo.

An amazing hold-up

OVERVIEW   Hold up water with a piece of cardboard — by reducing the pressure inside a glass.

MATERIALS
- a clear glass, or jar
- water
- scissors
- a sink or tub

- an index card or, piece of cardboard from a cereal box (large enough to completely cover the mouth of the jar)

PROCEDURES

1. Do this activity at a sink or tub.

2. Take an index card, or cut a piece of cardboard from a cereal box, large enough to completely cover the mouth of the glass.

3. Add some water to the glass.

4. Cover the mouth of the glass with the cardboard.
- Hold the cardboard in place with the palm of your hand.

5. Invert the glass.

6. Slowly move away the hand that is holding the cardboard.

RESULT

The cardboard didn't fall. Instead it held the water in the upside down glass.

IF IT DOESN'T WORK

If the cardboard doesn't hold on your first attempt, make sure it is thoroughly soaked. By wetting the cardboard it forms a better seal with the rim of the glass.

WHAT'S HAPPENING?

The cardboard seals the water and air in the glass. The only way for it to fall off is to let some air in. Without air moving into the glass, water can't move out. In other words, atmospheric pressure is pushing up on the cardboard with greater pressure than the water can press down. Make a small pin hole, or tilt the glass enough to open the edge of the cardboard, and the water falls out.

What else?

◎ After the cardboard is well soaked, try gently turning the glass upright and upside down without supporting the cardboard with your hand. Can you move the glass around without having the water spill out?

Trick your friends 15

OVERVIEW   Play this trick on your friends at a swimming pool, tub, or kitchen sink.

MATERIALS
- *At a pool:* use a small pail or pot, and newspaper
- *At a sink:* use a tall unbreakable glass, and paper towel
- water

PROCEDURES

1. Jam a wad of newspaper into the bottom of the pail.

- Jam it in so tight that it won't fall out when you hold the pail upside down.

2. Now jump in the pool... *Better change into a bathing suit first.*

3. Hold the pail upside down, and lower it into the water.

- If you didn't figure out before why we specified "small" pail, it will be obvious now.

- Trying to push a big bucket underwater is hard. For a five gallon bucket, you'd have to push down with forty pounds of force.

RESULTS

As long as you were able to keep the pail from tilting to one side, the paper inside will be dry.

WHAT'S HAPPENING?

The air inside the pail or glass can't escape (unless there is a leak in the pail) and it takes up space, keeping the water away from the paper. However, if you tried this in the ocean and lowered the pail a few hundred feet, the air inside would have been compressed by the huge water pressures. Water would have risen inside as the air took up less room, and the paper would have gotten soaked.

DEMONSTRATION TIP

❖ *Challenge your friends to push the pot underwater without getting the paper wet. When they say it's impossible, tell them you can do it without a problem. Go ahead, be a showoff.*

Bend light 16 with a glass of water

OVERVIEW Water bends light and you can see the effect.

MATERIALS
- a tall clear glass
- a straw or pencil
- water

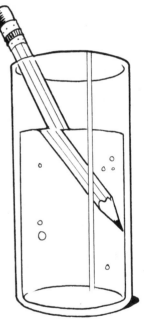

PROCEDURES

1. Fill the glass 2/3 full of water.

2. Drop in the straw or pencil.

3. Look at the glass from the side. Does it look like the pencil is broken?

WHAT'S HAPPENING

You see the pencil because it reflects light toward your eyes. The reflected light passing through the water is bent, while the light passing through air isn't. At the water surface you see where the two images come together, the straight image and the bent one. It looks like the pencil is broken.

17 Pour a glass of light

OVERVIEW   You can "pour" light when you shine a flashlight through a stream of water, which acts like an optical fiber.

MATERIALS
- a darkened room
- jar with screw-on lid
- hammer
- large and small nails
- flashlight
- hole punch
- masking tape
- newspaper
- bucket
- water
- cardboard
- scissors

CONSTRUCTION

1. Take the lid off the jar. Using the hammer and a large nail, make a hole near the rim.

2. Using the hammer and a small nail, punch a hole through the lid on the opposite side.

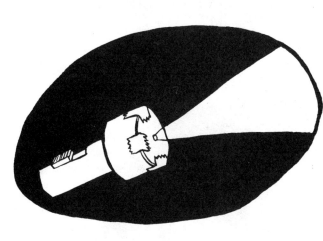

3. Make a flashlight cover:

- Trace the end of the flashlight onto the cardboard.
- Cut out the shape.
- Use a hole punch to make a very small hole or a narrow slit in the center.
- Tape it onto the light-emitting end of the flashlight.
- Turn on the flashlight and make sure light comes only from the small hole. Turn off the flashlight.

4. Fill the jar with water and screw on the lid.

5. Wrap the sides of the jar in several sheets of newspaper to block light from entering from the sides. Leave enough paper at the bottom of the jar so it will cover the front of the flashlight.

6. Darken the room. Turn on the flashlight and insert it into the newspaper so it shines into the bottom of the jar.

ACTION In the darkened room, pour water from the larger of the two holes in the lid.

RESULTS You can see the bright light captured in the stream of water. You're "pouring," or redirecting, light.

WHAT'S HAPPENING? Normally we think of light as traveling in straight lines. However, light *can* curve. In this case, once light enters the water stream it bounces (reflects) off the sides so it stays in the stream even as the stream bends. This is how optical fibers work. Like the stream of water, optical fibers keep reflecting the light internally so it can't escape. Optical fibers are replacing metal wires in carrying telephone messages and computer communications.

What else?

Try interrupting the stream of water and light by blocking it with your hand.

Try different sizes & shapes for the hole in the flashlight cover to see which works best.

~ PART THREE ~
BUILDING BOATS, SUBS, WATER WHEELS, & MORE

Making boats

OVERVIEW   You can make flat bottom boats or "V" hull boats out of materials you recycle and experience buoyancy.

MATERIALS
- quart or half gallon size milk or juice carton
- scissors
- duct tape

- a swimming pool, pond, or tub
- water
- nails, pennies, pebbles

CONSTRUCTION

1. Decide which boat you will make and then cut the milk or juice carton.

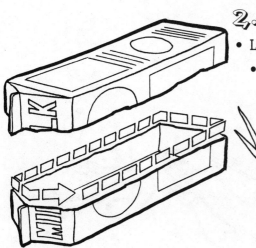

2. To make a flat bottom boat:
- Lay a carton on its side on a work bench.
- Cut along the middle of one side
- Cut across the bottom.
- Cut along the middle of the other side.
- Finally cut the top edge.
- Now, you have two hulls.

3. To make "V" hulls:

• Cut along one corner edge.

• Cut diagonally across the bottom.

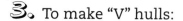

• Cut along the edge on the opposite side of your first cut.

• You will want to add some "ballast" or weight to the bottom of the "V" hulls. In a boat or ship the keel is weighted to keep it upright.

• Tape shut the "bow" or front end of your model to keep out water.

ACTION

Try floating your models in a swimming pool, pond, or tub. See how much weight they will hold by dropping in nails, pennies, or other weights. What happens when the hull is depressed so far that water comes over the side? Ever get that sinking feeling?

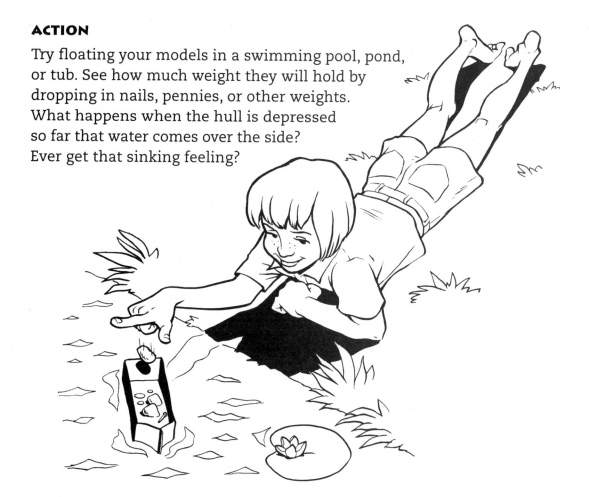

Even though you add weight to your boat, it still weighs less than the water it's pushing aside. However, when you keep adding weight and water starts pouring in over the sides of the boat, it becomes heavier than the water it displaces and sinks to the bottom. When the boat is floating, we say it has *positive buoyancy*: water is pushing it upward more than gravity is pulling it down.

What else?

◎ How could you propel your boat?
  Check out the chapters that follow for some ideas.

◎ What else could you convert into a model boat?
  Walnut shells? Two-liter bottles? Boards? Styrene trays?

Balloon power  19

OVERVIEW   Make any of the following models using balloons for propulsion.

MATERIALS
- a milk carton boat (Project 18) or a paper plate
- two bendable straws
- a balloon
- a paper clip
- duct tape
- a nail
- stapler
- swimming pool, or tub filled with water

CONSTRUCTION   This propulsion system can drive boats made of a variety of materials: milk cartons, paper plates, or styrene trays. Once you have the hull made, you can start on the propulsion system described below.

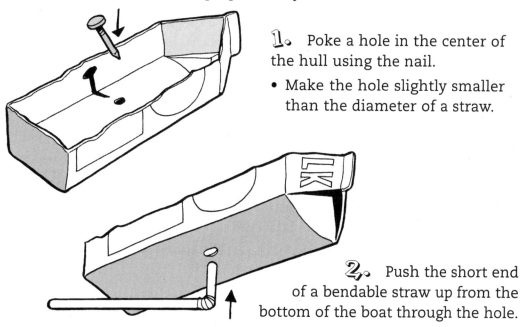

1. Poke a hole in the center of the hull using the nail.
- Make the hole slightly smaller than the diameter of a straw.

2. Push the short end of a bendable straw up from the bottom of the boat through the hole.

3. Bend the long end of the straw so it points opposite to the direction you want the boat to travel.

- Tape it in place against the bottom of the hull.

4. Cut a 4" section of another straw to insert into the mouth of the balloon.

- Tape it in place so it will won't leak air.

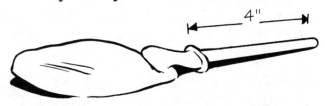

ACTION

Inflate the balloon by blowing through the section of the straw taped to the balloon. When the balloon is inflated, jam the end of the straw into the opening of the straw sticking up from the boat hull. Let air out of the balloon as you launch the boat in a tub or pool.

RESULTS

The boat will move across the tub,
propelled by air pressure in the balloon.

What else?

◎ Do *two* balloons push your boat *twice* as far?

Give it a try.

WHAT'S HAPPENING?

You used energy to inflate the balloon. Energy is stored in the inflated balloon as air at higher pressure. When the higher pressure air is released, it leaves the straw and pushes water in one direction which propels the boat in the opposite direction. This is just like skating: when you want to go forward, you push backward.

PUTT-PUTT

Make one change to your boat to give it a neat sound and help it travel farther.

- Use a stapler to restrict the air coming out of the straw.
- Staple the end of the submerged straw by putting the staple parallel to the straw.
- If that doesn't constrict the straw enough, pinch it further with a paper clip.
- When you release the air in the balloon, the boat will "putt-putt" through the water.

PADDLE BOAT

You can propel your boat with rubber bands instead of a balloon. Build a paddle out of two rectangles you cut from the sides of a quart milk carton.

- Slit the rectangles in the middle so they can fit together to form an "X."
- Tape two 6" long dowels along the sides of your boat, extending 3" behind the stern.
- Loop a rubber band around the paddle and onto each dowel. Wind up the paddle to make the boat go.
- Which way are you winding it?

Electric boat  20

OVERVIEW Build a boat that is powered by a battery. This project is fun because you can easily reconfigure the propeller to make the boat go faster, slower, forward, or backward.

MATERIALS
- a small electric motor (available at hobby stores)
- a styrene tray
- duct tape
- clear tape
- a coffee stirrer
- aluminum foil
- fast drying glue
- rubber band
- two large paper clips
- nail or sharp pencil
- a "D" cell battery

CONSTRUCTION

1. Form the propeller from a piece of aluminum foil.

- Cut a piece about 3" long and 1" wide.
- Fold it in half each direction so it's about 1 1/2" long and 1/2" wide.

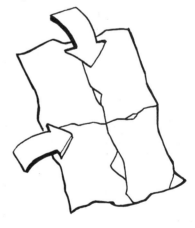

- With a nail or sharp pencil, punch a small hole in the center.
- Fit the coffee stirrer through the hole and glue in place.
- Let this dry.

2. While the glue is drying, prepare the battery.

- Jam the large loop of one paper clip onto the knob on one end of the battery. Close the loop to hold it tight.
- Hold the other paper clip on the flat end of the battery and loop a rubber band around both paper clips to hold them in place.

3. Jab the end of the coffee stirrer through the end of the boat (styrene tray).

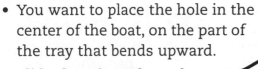

- You want to place the hole in the center of the boat, on the part of the tray that bends upward.
- Slide the stirrer through the hole so its free end is near the battery.

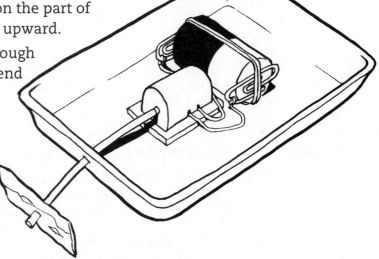

4. Cut a tiny piece of clear tape and wrap it around the motor shaft.

- Slide the coffee stirrer onto the shaft. If this isn't a tight fit, use a slightly larger piece of clear tape on the shaft. An alternative method is to glue the stirrer onto the shaft.

5. Use a narrow piece of duct tape to secure the electric motor to the styrene tray.

- Because you will want the heavy battery to sit in the middle of the boat (for balance), you should tape the motor just aft of that.

6. If the glue has dried holding the aluminum foil to the stirrer, carefully twist the foil.

- Hold each end between a thumb and forefinger and twist them in opposite directions.

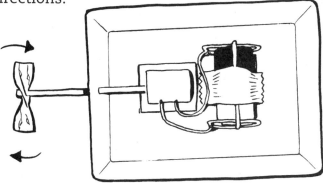

7. You're ready to hook up the battery to the motor.

- Slide one wire between the metal pieces of one paper clip.
- Repeat for the other wire on the other end of the battery.
- The motor should start to turn

ACTION

Place the boat into some water. What happens? If it goes backwards, you can switch leads on the battery. Or, with the motor stopped, twist the propeller in the opposite direction.

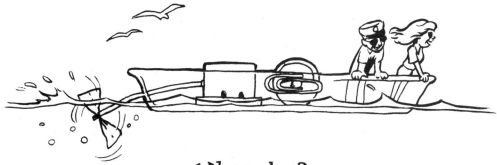

What else?

◎ Once you've got the boat working, try using more and less twist on the propeller to see what makes it go faster.
You could also try smaller and larger propellers.

WHAT'S HAPPENING?

You're using the energy stored in the battery to power the electric motor and it turns the shaft and the propeller, which pushes the boat.

MORE POWER

If you want to turn the propeller faster, hook up another battery in series. Use the paper clips and a piece of wire to connect the positive end of one battery to the negative end of the other (look for symbols "+" and "−" on the battery). Then connect the motor to the ends of the two batteries that aren't connected to each other.

SCIENCE FAIR

- You could run experiments with different lengths of propeller. Time how long it takes the boat to travel the length of a tub or pool. Change propellers and repeat the experiment.

  - You could graph the length of the propeller against the speed (distance divided by time) of travel.

  - You would want to try at least three more different propellers. What size propeller is best?

  - Another experiment would be to see how the speed increases as you add a second or a third battery. Do you expect the speed to increase the same amount every time you add a battery? Why?

  - Instead of using a styrene tray, use a half gallon milk container. Cut it in half, lengthwise, from corner to corner to give a "V" hull. This will let you place the propeller below the water level.

Dive, 21 dive, dive

OVERVIEW Build a submarine that lets you change its buoyancy and sink or swim.

MATERIALS
- an empty 1 to 1.5 liter water bottle with lid
- duct tape
- plastic or rubber tubing, 1/4" diameter, 3' long (from a hardware store)
- a nail
- long bolt, or metal weight
- glue
- round file
- swimming pool, or tub filled with water

CONSTRUCTION

To make a model submarine rise and fall in the water, you need to make a way to get air and water into and out of the submarine. More air inside and it rises; more water inside and down she goes.

1. Using the nail, carefully punch four holes in a straight line along the length of the bottle. Make these holes up to 1/4" in diameter.

2. Tape the long bolt along the side where you punched the holes. The weight will be the keel of the submarine, keeping it right side up.

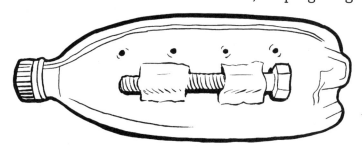

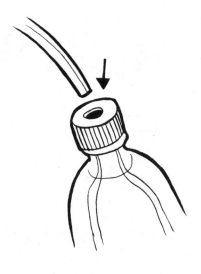

3. Again using the nail, make a hole in the lid of the bottle.

- It will be easier and safer to have the lid screwed onto the bottle while you make the hole.

- You will want to make the hole barely large enough to squeeze in the rubber or plastic tubing.

- If it's not big enough, enlarge the hole with a round file.

4. When you can jam the tubing into the lid, glue it in place.

ACTION

Place the submarine in a swimming pool or tub. It should float with the keel down. To get it to dive, suck air out of the bottle through the tubing. Once submerged, it will resurface when you blow air back into the sub through the tube.

WHAT'S HAPPENING?

The bottle full of water will sink. Even a small amount of air will keep it afloat at the surface. The air provides buoyancy to balance the weight of the keel. As you blow in more air, the submarine will ride higher out of the water.

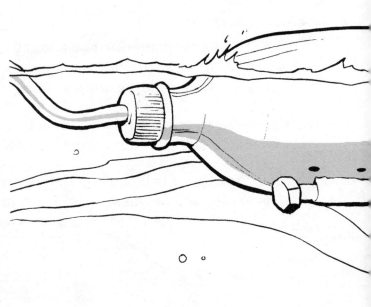

WET & WACKY FACTS

*Think submarines are a new development in ships?
The first one was made 380 years ago by covering a wood boat
with animal hides. Care to go for a deep dive in that?*

*How deep can a submarine go?
Not deeper than the bottom of the ocean.
The research submersible* **Trieste** *reached
the deepest spot in the world ocean, 35,800' deep.*

22 Waterwheels and turbines

OVERVIEW   Spin a waterwheel by having water flow from inside a bottle to outside.

MATERIALS
- 2-liter soda bottle
- scissors
- a nail, or hole punch
- 3' long string

- 12" long vinyl hose, $3/8$" inner diameter or larger (from a hardware store)
- running water from a hose, or bath tub

PROCEDURES

1. Cut the top off a 2-liter soda bottle and use a nail or hole punch to make three equally spaced holes near the top.

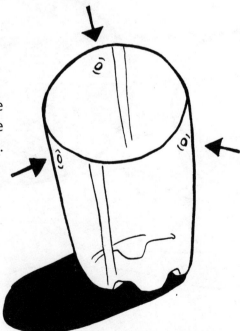

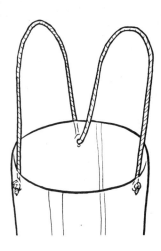

2. Tie the end of a 3' long piece of string through one hole, and run the free end through the next hole and tie it at the third hole.

- You can hold the bottle up by raising the two loops of string.

3. Cut the vinyl hose into three pieces about 4" long.

4. Use the nail to poke three holes in the side of the bottle, as close to the bottom as you can.

- These should be equally spaced around the bottle.

5. Use scissors to enlarge the holes so a piece of vinyl hose will fit securely in each hole.

- Bend the hose so all three pieces curve in the same direction.

ACTION

Hold up the bottle by the string so that one hand is holding both loops, and pour in water to fill the bottle. It will start to spin.

Or, you could tie a string or swivel to the two loops that will allow the turbine to spin.

RESULTS You've made a turbine.

IF IT DOESN'T WORK

Make sure water leaving the vinyl hose is moving sideways, and that all three water streams are in the same direction. To reduce the effect of twisting the string, tie a swivel (from a fisherman's tackle box) to a string holding the two loops supporting the bottle and hold onto the other end of the swivel.

WET & WACKY FACTS

What would you guess is the largest waterwheel?
The record is 130' in diameter.
You'd need a big river to move that wheel.

WHAT'S HAPPENING?

This turbine is being turned by the water pressure
at the bottom of the bottle. If the bottle were taller,
which would let you pour in more water and
increase the pressure, it would spin faster.

SCIENCE FAIR

- You could test different arrangements of hose to see which made the most revolutions in a minute.

- You could test different diameter hose from drinking straws to the largest hose you can find. Or, you could use one size hose and increase the number of ports you make.

- Graph the hose size against number of spins, or the number of ports against the number of spins per minute to show what the optimum arrangement is. Mark the bottle in one place to help you count the number of spins.

Whirlpool in a bottle 23

OVERVIEW You can build a simple gizmo that will let you make whirlpools in a bottle. Spinning helps water drain from one bottle to another by allowing air to replace escaping water.

MATERIALS
- two 2-liter soda bottles
- a metal washer, 1" diameter with a $1/2$" opening
- water
- duct tape

PROCEDURES

1. Remove the wrappings from each bottle so you can see inside.

2. Fill one bottle about half or two thirds full of water.

3. Rest the metal washer on top of the bottle containing water, centering it on the opening.

4. Hold the second bottle on top of the first one so the openings are aligned.

5. Using 6" of duct tape, tape the two bottles together where they touch, making sure the washer is held in place between the two.

ACTION Invert the two bottles holding one hand on the bottle with water and the other hand firmly gripping the two bottle necks. Swirl the upper bottle to get the water spinning in one direction. Once it's spinning, rest the bottom bottle on a counter and watch the whirlpool form. If water leeks out, retape the two bottles together.

RESULTS You've created a whirlpool!

WHAT'S HAPPENING? Although you started with a fairly slow rotation of water in the bottle, it was spinning much faster as the last of it drained into the lower bottle. As water started to spin around inside the bottle, some water drained into the lower bottle which extended the swirling. As the whirlpool got longer, it spun faster.

ANOTHER EXPERIMENT Try draining the bottle that has the water without swirling. How fast does the water flow into the lower bottle? Do you see bubbles rising into the higher bottle? What's going on?

WHAT'S HAPPENING?

The whirlpool lets air move from the lower bottle to the upper bottle to replace the volume of water that's falling into the lower bottle. When you don't swirl the bottles, air can't escape the lower bottle as easily. A little water flows into the lower bottle and then a burp of air escapes as a bubble into the upper bottle. Then, some more water can fall. If you could stop the burp from happening, would water flow into the lower bottle?

Hit the Showers

Does it matter which way you spin the whirlpool bottle?
No, you could be make it work either direction.
Check out the flow of water down the drain in your tub or sink.
Which way does it go? Lots of people will tell you
it will spin clockwise in the Northern Hemisphere
and counterclockwise in the Southern Hemisphere.
Not true. Try swishing the water in your tub
and you'll see you can get it to spin in either direction.
Your location has nothing to do with what direction it spins
any more than it did in the bottle.

24 Send a note in a bottle

OVERVIEW Use ocean currents to deliver a note to someone you don't know. Maybe they will send a note back to you and you can see which way the currents took the bottle.

MATERIALS
- an empty plastic soda drink bottle with a screw on lid
- a self-addressed, stamped postcard
- some beach sand
- candle wax (optional)

CONSTRUCTION

1. Print your name and address on the postcard and put on a stamp.

- On the message side, write a note asking the finder to please send the postcard to you, and to indicate where and when they found the bottle.

- The finder might want to know where and when you launched it, so include that information.

- Make sure you thank them.

2. Roll the card up so it fits into the bottle.

3. Add about 2" of dry sand. The sand will weight the bottle down so the wind won't be able to push it. You'll find out where ocean currents took the bottle and not the wind.

4. Screw on the lid tightly.

- You can dip the cap end of the bottle in melted candle wax to protect it from corroding in the ocean, or try your bottle without this step.

ACTION
Get some adult help to launch your bottle.
Try to get it tossed beyond the breakers at the beach.

WET & WACKY FACTS
The longest recorded trip

for a note in a bottle is 73 years.
Hopefully yours will be found faster than that.

IF IT DOESN'T WORK

Your bottle may sink and never be found, or someone could find it and not send back your card. Be patient and hopeful. You could launch several at the same time to increase the odds that one will be found. This is what oceanographers do when they study surface currents.

POLLUTION ALERT

Your science project may be someone else's pollution. Don't launch more than a few bottles because no one wants more litter on our beaches.

RESULTS

If you get your postcard back, check the launch and recovery locations on a map. How far apart are the locations? How long did it take for the bottle to get there? Of course the bottle may have been on the beach for days before being found, but assuming it just arrived the day it was found, how fast were the ocean currents?

WHAT'S HAPPENING?

You won't know what path the bottle took to get to its recovery beach, but you do know that currents carried it there. In different times of the year, the bottle may travel in different directions or go much faster or slower. It could even go in the opposite direction.

What else?

◎ Try running the experiment in winter and summer to see if you get the same result. If the currents are different in winter and summer, what do you suppose makes them different?

Make a 25 water magnifier

OVERVIEW   Make a magnifier lens with water and see how a lens works.

MATERIALS
- a 2-liter clear plastic bottle with the lid
- clear plastic wrap
- scissors
- rubber band
- water
- a sink
- a piece of newspaper

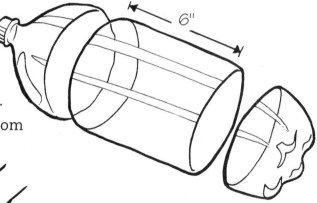

CONSTRUCTION

1. Cut a 6" long section from the center of the plastic bottle.

- Cut off both the top and bottom leaving a cylinder 6" long.

2. Rip a square piece of plastic wrap and lay it over one end of the cylinder.

3. Carefully push a finger down the center of the plastic wrap to make a 1" depression.

4. Place the rubber band around the cylinder to hold the plastic wrap in place.

5. Pour some water onto the plastic wrap. Best to do this over a sink.

6. Put the piece of newspaper, or other object to view onto the top of the lid. Lift the cylinder over the lid and let it rest on the counter.

- Try raising and lowering the cylinder to get it into better focus.
- You could also try adding more water to the lens.

ACTION   Look from above the cylinder through the pocket of water at the newspaper print on the lid.

RESULTS   The type will appear larger when viewed through the magnifier.

WHAT'S HAPPENING?

Water causes light to bend, just as the lens in a magnifying glass does (*see* Project 16). The lens bends light reflected from the object toward your eye making it appear to be larger than it is.

ANOTHER EXPERIMENT

- Grab another 2-liter bottle or a tall, clear glass and fill with water.
- Prop the front page of the newspaper or other large print against a wall and place the filled bottle about 8" away.
- Look through the bottle, keeping your eyes level with the bottle and print. The print will be inverted.
- Move the bottle closer to the print. At about 4" away you'll see the print normally, but magnified.
- Try other glasses to see how they work.

WHAT'S HAPPENING?

The water in the bottle acts like a lens and bends light. At distances of about 8" the light is bent so far that the image appears to be reversed, the right side of the image appears to be on the left.

26 Making an underwater viewer

OVERVIEW   Did you lose something underwater? Make an underwater viewing scope to help you find it. Or, to find where the fish are.

MATERIALS
- a 2-liter bottle
- scissors
- clear plastic wrap
- rubber band
- swimming pool, or pond

CONSTRUCTION

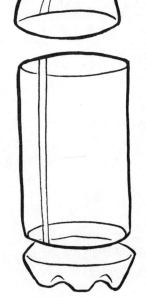

1. Cut off the top end of the bottle.
- Carefully poke one end of the scissors into the bottle at the top of the straight section. Cut around the bottle to remove the top.

2. Use the same procedure as in step 1 to remove the bottom of the bottle.

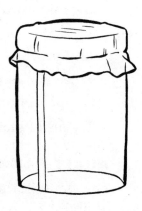

3. Tear off a square piece of clear plastic wrap and lay it on one end of the cylinder you made from the bottle.
- Stretch it tightly over the end of the bottle and use the rubber band to hold the wrap in place.
- Make sure the plastic wrap has a smooth surface and that the rubber band makes a tight fit.

ACTION   Push the end covered in plastic wrap into a pond or pool and look through the other end. Compare your view with and without the underwater viewing scope.

RESULTS   The viewing scope helps you see underwater.

WHAT'S HAPPENING?

The viewer reduces the amount of light reflecting off the surface of the water and hitting your eye which makes it easier to see.

What else?

◎ Try making a really long underwater viewer. Use a long section of PVC pipe. The trick will be to get the plastic wrap to stay in place in the deeper water (higher pressure). Try using duct tape to hold the wrap.

27 Make a water clock

OVERVIEW   Keep time in a bottle! But eventually it drips away.

MATERIALS
- several 2-liter plastic bottles, or plastic cartons
- a small nail
- masking tape
- pencil
- bendable straws
- water
- paper clips
- kitchen timer, or watch with a second hand

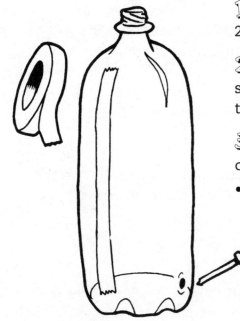

CONSTRUCTION

1. Punch a nail hole in the bottom of a 2-liter bottle or other plastic container.

2. Put a piece of masking tape on the side of the bottle so it extends from near the bottom of the bottle to the top.

3. Fill the bottle with water while covering the hole you made.
- Have someone mark the water level on the masking tape with a pencil.

4. Let the water escape through the hole while you keep time.
- Mark the water level on the masking tape every minute.

ACTION

With the water levels marked on the side of the bottle, you've made a clock. Refill the bottle to one of the marks and you can use it as a timer. You could fill in more marks on the side of the bottle to indicate quarter and half minute intervals to be more precise.

WHAT'S HAPPENING?

You may have noticed that the water flowed out of the hole fastest when the bottle was fullest, and it slowed down as the water level decreased. The less pressure pushing water out, the slower it emptied.

However, as long as you use the same water level each time, the marks you made on the side of the bottle will give you accurate time intervals.

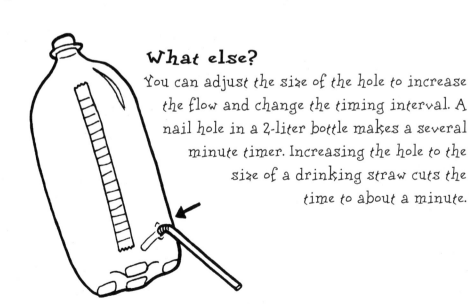

What else?

You can adjust the size of the hole to increase the flow and change the timing interval. A nail hole in a 2-liter bottle makes a several minute timer. Increasing the hole to the size of a drinking straw cuts the time to about a minute.

COMPLEX CLOCKS

Want to measure longer time? You can set up several water clocks that drip into one another to record longer time intervals. If you can set up your monster clock on some outside stairs where they won't be in people's way, build the following clock.

1. In the side of a 2-liter bottle make a hole barely large enough to squeeze in a drinking straw.

• Force the longer end of a bendable straw into the hole.

2. Bend the short end down so it will drain into the top of a second 2-liter bottle on the step below.

3. Make a hole in the second bottle and insert a straw as in step 1.

4. Fill the top bottle and time how long it takes for the bottom bottle to drain.

• If you want the clock to run slower, pinch the straw draining the first bottle with a paper clip.

What else?

◎ Instead of using stairs, you could mount the bottles upside down on a fence post or a piece of wood. Cut off the bottoms of all the bottles. Make the holes in the lids so water can drain out and into the next upside bottle.

WET & WACKY FACTS

Egyptians were using water clocks 3,400 years ago. A thousand years later Plato of Athens, Greece invented a water alarm clock. Maybe it soaked you if you overslept?

5. You can continue adding bottles to your clock placing one on each of the stairs.

• You will have to extend the straws to make them reach the next bottle. To do this, insert the end of one straw into another.

Crossword puzzle glossary

ACROSS

1. To sip your soda, you reduce this at the top of the straw (*Hint: Project 7*)

2. Sprays droplets of liquid when you force air through it (*Hint: Project 8*)

4. Weight you add to a boat to help keep it upright (*Hint: Project 18*)

6. Water molecules stick together with surface _____ (*Hint: Project 2*)

7. A web-footed, fish-eating, diving bird (*Hint: Part one*)

8. A machine spun by moving water (*Hint: Project 22*)

9. Upward pressure exerted by water (*Hint: Project 18*)

DOWN

1. Pushes boats (*Hint: Project 20*)

3. Moves water from higher containers to lower containers (*Hint: Project 7*)

5. The weight of a material divided by the volume it occupies (*Hint: Part one*)

7. You can make one with water to bend light (*Hint: Project 25*)

• *Solution to the puzzle on the copyright page in the front of this book (page iv)*

88